21st Century Skills **INNOVATION** *Library*

From Locusts to . . . Automobile Anti-Collision Systems

by Wil Mara

Published in the United States of America by Cherry Lake Publishing
Ann Arbor, Michigan
www.cherrylakepublishing.com

Content Adviser: Mariappan Jawaharlal, PhD, Professor of Mechanical Engineering, California State
Polytechnic University, Pomona, California

Design: The Design Lab

Photo Credits: Cover and page 3, ©Theo Gottwald/Dreamstime.com; cover inset, ©Jakub
Kozak/Shutterstock, Inc.; page 4, ©Dmitry Dedyukhin/Dreamstime.com; page 6, ©Jim West/
Alamy; page 7, ©Uatp1/Dreamstime.com; page 9, ©Zoom-zoom/Dreamstime.com; page 10,
©Excitations/Alamy; page 13, ©Nigel Cattlin/Alamy; page 14, ©vvoe/Shutterstock, Inc.; page 17,
©Waymoreawesomer/Dreamstime.com; page 18, ©iStockphoto.com/gehringj; page 19,
©culture-images GmbH/Alamy; page 20, ©Rihardzz/Shutterstock, Inc.; page 21, ©Zurijeta/
Shutterstock, Inc.; page 22, ©gemphotography/Shutterstock, Inc.; page 24, ©iStockphoto.
com/kevdog818; page 25, ©sonya etchison/Shutterstock, Inc.; page 27, ©Stefano Panzeri/
Shutterstock, Inc.; page 28, ©c./Shutterstock, Inc.

Library of Congress Cataloging-in-Publication Data
Mara, Wil.
 From locusts to – automobile anti-collision systems/by Wil Mara.
    p. cm.–(Innovations from nature) (Innovation library)
 Includes bibliographical references and index.
 Audience: Grade 4 to 6.
 ISBN 978-1-61080-501-8 (lib. bdg.) – ISBN 978-1-61080-588-9 (e-book) –
ISBN 978-1-61080-675-6 (pbk.)
 1. Automobiles–Collision avoidance systems. 2. Locusts. 3. Biomimicry. I. Title.
TL272.52.M37 2012
629.2'76–dc23   2012011856

Cherry Lake Publishing would like to acknowledge
the work of The Partnership for 21st Century Skills.
Please visit www.21stcenturyskills.org for more information.

Printed in the United States of America
Corporate Graphics Inc.
July 2012
CLFA11

CONTENTS

Chapter One
**A Brief History of Automotive
      Safety**   **4**

Chapter Two
Focus on the Locust   **9**

Chapter Three
From There to Reality   **14**

Chapter Four
The Road Ahead   **20**

Chapter Five
The Brightest Minds   **25**

Glossary   30
For More Information   31
Index   32
About the Author   32

CHAPTER ONE

A Brief History of Automotive Safety

Car crashes can cause serious injuries to drivers and passengers.

Have you ever seen or been in a car accident? It's one of the most frightening experiences you can imagine. The screeching of tires, the crunching of metal, and the shattering of glass can scare even the bravest people. A person can be badly injured in a car crash, and some even die. Roughly 10 million car accidents occur every year in the United States. Automobile accidents cost lives, time, energy, and money. Wouldn't it be great if there was some kind of technology that could reduce the number of car accidents?

The first true automobile to run under its own power was a steam-driven tricycle built around 1770. The first practical vehicle to have a gasoline-powered engine was built in Germany in 1885. By this time, the first auto-related death had already occurred. In 1869, Irish scientist Mary Ward was thrown from a steam-powered vehicle as it went around a curve. Ward fell under the car's wheels, was run over, and died almost instantly. She was the world's first known victim of a car accident.

By the early 1930s, many people in the United States were pushing for better safety standards in cars, including cushions on dashboards and seat belts. The first **air bag** was introduced in the early 1950s, although the technology to use them properly would not be developed until the next decade. Finally, in the 1970s, car manufacturers began equipping new vehicles with

Learning & Innovation Skills

Having developed roll cages, seat belts, and air bags, you'd think the experts had considered everything possible to make driving safer. But had they thought about color? According to studies made in the last 10 years, the color of a car can actually affect the chances of it getting into an accident. Researchers have found that black cars have a greater risk than all others. Other high-risk colors include brown, green, gray, silver, red, and blue. The lowest-risk colors are white and pink.

air bags. In the 1980s, most states began adopting laws requiring people to wear seat belts.

In the late 1950s, the United Nations began a worldwide effort to promote auto safety. One of its most important developments was the roll cage. This

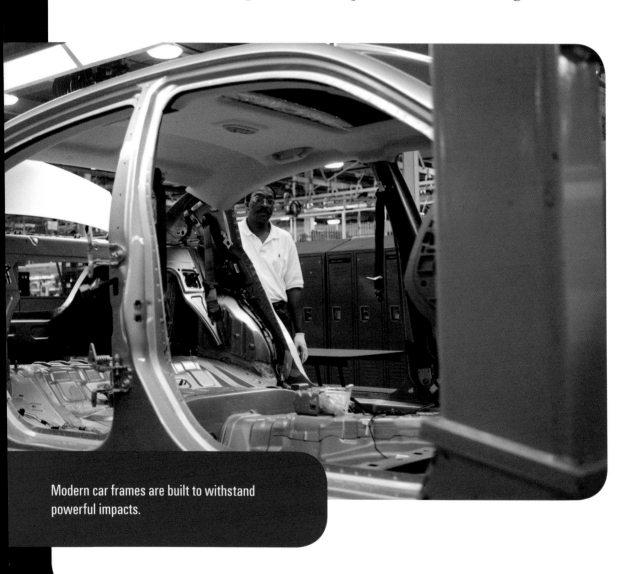

Modern car frames are built to withstand powerful impacts.

Auto manufacturers use human-shaped dummies to test how different types of crashes will affect people in vehicles.

was a tough "shell" of connected pipes that was set inside a vehicle's outer body. The shell could withstand tremendous impact. It gave people inside the vehicle extra protection.

In the 1960s, the U.S. government established the Department of Transportation. In the 1970s, it launched the National Highway Traffic Safety Administration. These agencies conducted **crash tests** to determine the safety level of many automobile makes and models. The results of the tests led to the creation of new or improved safety devices and new car designs.

In time, experts came to believe a new technology was needed that would help to avoid crashes in the first place. Amazingly, the key to this new technology was found not in a laboratory or on a test course, but in the wild world of insects.

CHAPTER TWO

Focus on the Locust

The technology used to minimize auto accidents is known as a **collision avoidance system** (CAS). This technology is based on the concept of **biomimicry**. In simple terms, biomimicry is the practice of copying nature—animals and plants—to build or improve something. It is becoming one of the most rapidly growing scientific fields in the world.

Many modern vehicles are equipped with collision avoidance systems to help drivers prevent crashes.

Locusts travel together in massive groups called swarms.

The animal that has provided the best inspiration for collision avoidance is an insect known as a **locust**. A locust is a type of grasshopper that flies in huge groups known as **swarms**. A swarm can travel long distances and move at great speeds. Locust swarms often destroy large areas of cropland and can cause entire communities to suffer severe food shortages.

In the early 1990s, Dr. Claire Rind, a biologist at Newcastle University in England, began taking an interest in locusts. She was particularly curious about their ability to travel in giant swarms without flying into each other or anything that came into their path. The ability of several million locusts to make a sudden left or right turn got her thinking: perhaps these creatures held the secret to avoiding car collisions. If so, could their unique ability be adapted into automobile design?

Like most insects, locusts can see many more images per second than humans can. This means they can react more quickly to things that are approaching very rapidly. To help an organism react to what it senses, many living creatures have cells called **neurons**. Neurons carry information between the brain and other parts of the organism's body. When a locust sees an oncoming object, a neuron rapidly sends messages to the rest of its body. These messages tell the insect to move out of the object's way.

Learning & Innovation Skills

 Locust-inspired collision avoidance systems aren't the only example of biomimicry that have been successfully adapted into everyday life. Another is the famous high-speed bullet train that was first built in Japan. The long, pointed shape of the train's nose is based on the beak of a bird known as a kingfisher. This bird can dive into water with almost no noise or resistance. Another biomimicry-inspired invention is the Fastskin swimsuit, which is based on the texture of a shark's skin. And the small light-reflecting studs you see on a road at night are based on the reflective eyes of a cat.

The locust then responds with equally amazing speed. The entire process of warning and then responding takes about 45-thousandths of a second! Scientists call the neuron that triggers this process the lobula giant movement detector (LGMD).

Dr. Rind's research revealed that the LGMD was triggered mostly by the approach of birds. This is because locusts encounter birds more than any other animal. However, she wanted to test the functions of the LGMD under a different set of circumstances. She positioned a group of locusts in front of a movie screen and showed them scenes from *Star Wars* in which many spaceships were flying around. Some of the craft even seemed to be flying right at the locusts. Dr. Rind discovered that the locusts showed a more alarmed reaction during these instances. She believed she had found the secret for a collision avoidance system.

Locusts' incredible reflexes enable them to move out of the way of incoming objects.

CHAPTER THREE

From There to Reality

Crowded city areas present drivers with a much higher number of obstacles than most other places.

Experts from many different fields have contributed to the development of a collision avoidance system based on a locust's LGMD. These fields include automobile development, neurobiology, computer hardware and software, and optoelectronics, or electronic vision.

During the earliest CAS experiments, Dr. Rind and her team built a small, three-wheeled robot.

It had cameras for eyes and was placed on an **obstacle** course, where it avoided about 90 percent of all possible collisions. The results were encouraging. But Dr. Rind knew that conditions in a laboratory were different from those that a driver would encounter in a real-life situation. For example, in a real car on an actual road, a CAS would have to process hundreds of possible obstacles. Some would be large, and others would be small. They would also have different colors. Some would be moving, like another car or a person on a bicycle. Others, like a mailbox or a telephone pole, would not move.

A CAS works in three steps. First it collects information, then it analyzes the information, and finally it produces a response. The first step, collecting information, requires the CAS to get a sense of what obstacles are near a vehicle at any given moment. There are three methods that can be used to do this. First, radio waves can be sent out and bounced back to the CAS. Second, in a variation on radio waves, beams of light are sent out and reflected back. Third, a camera can be used to take pictures of nearby obstacles. Regardless of which method is used, **sensors** or tiny cameras must be positioned all around the vehicle.

The key to Dr. Rind's research is a computer chip that is used in the system. The chip is inspired by the

21st Century Content

Computers are becoming "smarter" all the time. A computer's greatest value lies in its ability to perform parallel processing, such as calculating numbers and demonstrating common logic. Today, programmers are trying to get computers to function in more abstract, human ways. For example, a computer may be able to analyze a painting and tell you what colors or what type of paints were used. But it cannot appreciate the painting's beauty or get a feel for its mood. Anyone interested in computer science would have a very bright future indeed if they could get computers to have these kinds of "emotional" responses.

locust's eye and is built to gather many images at once. The chip then sends the signals it has picked up to the CAS computer's "brain" to be analyzed. This is the second step of the process. The information is reviewed, and the system decides if a response is needed. This is probably the trickiest part of the CAS process. A computer must make a judgment equal to that of a human brain making an important decision. For example, a CAS might consider a traffic cone to be just as important as a small child since they are about the same size.

Engineers have struggled with making a CAS that can understand such differences and make lightning-fast judgments. To date, a CAS can determine whether an object is getting too close to a vehicle. But when it comes to the fine details, modern CASs still have some shortcomings.

A CAS can be very helpful for parking in tight spaces.

The third and final step of the process involves the response. A CAS can react to a possible problem in one of two ways: **passively** or **actively**. A passive response would not require the CAS to actually take control of a vehicle, whereas an active response would. A passive

Passive systems rely on the driver to react once the CAS gives a warning.

An active CAS would apply a vehicle's brakes before the driver even presses the pedal.

response could be a series of sounds or visual signals, such as blinking lights on the dashboard. These would alert the driver to a possible collision and give him or her time to respond. An active response might include applying the brakes, tightening the seat belts, or inflating the air bags.

CHAPTER FOUR

The Road Ahead

CASs have helped prevent many injuries and deaths.

It is believed that a reliable collision avoidance system will be able to prevent about 2 million accidents in the United States each year. Yet CASs still have a number of problems that need to be worked out before they can become standard equipment in every vehicle.

One challenge that CAS developers have encountered involves the different lighting conditions that a

CAS sensors must be able to adjust to rapid changes in lighting.

driver encounters, such as extreme darkness and extreme brightness. CAS sensors can adjust when someone is driving during the day or night. But what happens when a car enters a tunnel and very suddenly goes from bright

Learning & Innovation Skills

At first, CASs were thought to be ideal only for protecting people *inside* a vehicle. Some engineers, however, are now tinkering with the idea of adding features that protect people outside a vehicle as well. One is a series of sounds made by the vehicle that will alert nearby pedestrians if the vehicle is coming too close to them. Another is a bumper air bag, which serves the same purpose as an air bag inside the vehicle. A bumper air bag would pop out from the bumper, or fender, of the car. Ideally, it would provide a cushion to a pedestrian who was in the path of an oncoming vehicle.

to dark conditions? Sensors can take incorrect readings under these circumstances. Heavy snow, rain, or ice can also make it difficult for sensors to take accurate readings.

Engineers are concerned about how sensitive the sensors should really be. If a sensor triggers an alarm too often, a driver may begin to ignore it after a while. This would make for a very dangerous situation when a real emergency occurred. Engineers are also worried that drivers would begin to rely too much on the CAS and become lazy about safety.

Another challenge is finding a way to make CASs more affordable. At this time, even the most basic CAS can drive the price of a new car way up. In fact, CASs are only included in vehicles whose price tags are extremely high to begin with. As engineers continue to refine and improve CASs, they are hoping to make them less expensive. Their goal is to someday be able to include them in every vehicle regardless of cost.

Engineers hope that every car on the road will one day be equipped with a CAS.

While CASs certainly have a long way to go before they're perfected, there's little doubt that they are the wave of the future. In time, they'll save millions of lives. And to think, it all began with an insect.

One tiny insect was the inspiration behind a device that could save countless lives.

CHAPTER FIVE

The Brightest Minds

Many people have made important contributions to the worlds of automotive safety and biomimicry. Without these original thinkers, many of today's most useful inventions would not exist. Here are just a few major contributors who have made our lives safer and more enjoyable.

Thanks to biomimicry, riding in cars is safer than ever before.

Life & Career Skills

New technologies inspired by biomimicry are going to play an important role in the future. Many of these technologies will be "green friendly." These technologies will do little or no harm to the environment while providing benefits to millions of people. If you want to take part in this aspect of the Green Revolution, you should study the natural sciences. Employment opportunities can be found in environmental research, teaching, engineering, computer software and hardware design, and some areas of medicine.

Claire Rind is a biologist at Newcastle University. Dr. Rind continues to improve collision avoidance technology while working with one of the world's leading auto manufacturers. One of her main concerns is that modern CASs respond too slowly to the most critical emergency situations. She also works with colleagues in Spain and Hungary, all of whom are playing an important part in furthering this important research.

Leonardo da Vinci (1452–1519) was the Renaissance man who painted the *Mona Lisa* and *The Last Supper*. Da Vinci was also a sculptor, an engineer, a mathematician, a musician, a mapmaker, and an inventor. He loved nature, and spent many days wandering through forests and along rivers. He wrote down his observations and sketched pictures in notebooks. Da Vinci may have been one of the first

Leonardo da Vinci is remembered today as both a brilliant scientist and a remarkable artist.

people to believe that many problems could be solved through careful study of plants and animals. His notes and drawings on flying machines were largely inspired by his study of birds. He never managed to produce a working airplane, but he understood the basics of biomimicry and saw its potential in the development of flight.

Da Vinci drew plans for a flying machine based on his observation of birds.

Janine Benyus (1958–) is one of the world's leading authorities on biomimicry. A professor at the University of Montana, she has written many books on biomimicry and started two organizations. The Biomimicry Guild develops biomimicry-inspired products, and the nonprofit Biomimicry Institute promotes biomimicry worldwide. She has received many awards, including the 2009 Champion of the Earth Award from the United Nations Environmental Programme and the Rachel Carson Environmental Ethics Award. In 2007, *Time* magazine chose her as one of its Heroes of the Environment award winners.

Glossary

actively (AK-tiv-lee) energetically and busily involving effort and action

air bag (AIR bag) a bag in motor vehicles that automatically inflates during an accident to protect a driver or passenger

biomimicry (bye-oh-MI-mi-kree) the practice of copying nature in order to build or improve something

collision avoidance system (kuh-LIZH-uhn uh-VOID-uhns SIS-tuhm) a device used in motor vehicles to identify potential danger and prevent accidents before they happen

crash tests (KRASH TESTS) tests involving the collision of two or more vehicles to determine their strength in relation to the impact

locust (LOH-kuhst) a type of grasshopper that moves in huge swarms and destroys crops and vegetation

neurons (NOOR-ahnz) cells that carry information between the brain and other parts of the body

obstacle (AHB-stuh-kuhl) something that makes it difficult to do or achieve something

passively (PAS-iv-lee) not participating readily or actively

sensors (SEN-surz) instruments that can detect and measure changes and transmit the information to a controlling device

swarms (SWORMZ) large groups of insects that gather or move in large numbers

For More Information

BOOKS

Butterfield, Moira. *Inventions!* New York: Franklin Watts, 2012.

Gates, Phil. *Nature Got There First.* New York: Kingfisher, 2010.

Lee, Dora. *Biomimicry: Inventions Inspired by Nature.* Tonawanda, NY: Kids Can Press, 2011.

Powell, Jillian. *Traffic and Road Safety.* New York: Franklin Watts, 2009.

WEB SITES

Ask Nature—What Is Biomimicry?
www.asknature.org/article/view/what_is_biomimicry
Find out more about biomimicry, with examples, further links, and interesting video content.

Biomimcry Institute and Biomimcry Guild
www.biomimicry.net
Check out the latest news on the science of biomimicry, with links to other sites as well as information for those interested in choosing a career in the field.

Science a GoGo
www.scienceagogo.com/news/20000307201150data_trunc_sys.shtml
Check out this article to learn more about the locust-inspired CAS and find other links to interesting articles about biomimicry.

Index

air bags, 5–6, 19, 22

Benyus, Janine, 29
biomimicry, 9, 11, 12, 26,
27–28, 29
brakes, 19
bullet trains, 12
bumper air bags, 22

car accidents
car colors and, 5
crash tests, 8
deaths, 4, 5
frequency of, 4
cats, 12
collision avoidance
systems (CASs)
active response, 18, 19
alerts, 19, 22

computer chips, 15–16
cost, 22
experiments, 14–15
information analysis,
16
information collection,
15, 22
lighting conditions,
20–22
passive response,
18–19
response, 16, 18–19,
26
sensors, 15, 22
computers, 14, 15–16,
26

da Vinci, Leonardo,
26–28

Department of Transpor-
tation, 8

employment, 26

Fastskin swimsuits, 12

Green Revolution, 26

kingfishers, 12

laws, 6
lobula giant movement
detector
(LGMD), 12, 14
locusts
neurons, 11–12
swarms, 11
vision, 11, 16

National Highway Traffic
Safety Adminis-
tration, 8

pedestrians, 22

Rind, Claire, 11, 12, 14,
15, 26
roadstuds, 12
roll cages, 5, 6, 8

seat belts, 5, 6, 19
sharks, 12
Star Wars, 12

United Nations, 6, 29

Ward, Mary, 5

About the Author

Wil Mara is the award-winning author of more than 120 books, many of which are educational titles for young readers. More information about his work can be found at www.wilmara.com.